A CONCISE SUMMARY OF BRENE BROWN'S

Daring Greatly

...in 30 minutes

A 30 MINUTE EXPERT SUMMARY

GARAMOND
PRESS

CONTENTS

INTRODUCTION

Overview

Brené Brown believes that shame in various forms is what keeps people from being vulnerable. Shame leads to fear and disengagement, and disengagement in turn kills creativity, learning, and innovation. According to Brown, this vicious cycle creates a need for perfection, and that need in turn leads to the belief that nothing a person has or does will ever be enough. But Brown also believes that if people can learn to practice vulnerability, in spite of the discomfort and the uncertainty that often go with being vulnerable, they can find deeper connections with family members, friends, and coworkers—and, perhaps most important, they can establish compassionate and loving relationships with themselves.

About the Author

Brené Brown, PhD., LMSW, is a research professor in the Graduate College of Social Work at the University of Houston. Her other books include *The Gifts of Imperfection, I Thought It Was Just Me*, and *Connections*, a textbook. Brown's research has been recognized in the academic world as well as by the general public. Her work has been featured on PBS, CNN, and NPR, and she appeared as a guest on *Katie*, the talk show hosted by Katie Couric on the ABC television network. In addition, Brown has made two TED Talks presentations; her first, "The Power of Vulnerability," is one of the most popular talks of the series, and, together with her second presentation, has attracted more than five million views on YouTube. Brown lives in Houston with her husband, Steve, and their two children, Ellen and Charlie.

How the Book Came About

Brené Brown spent ten years conducting research on vulnerability, interviewing more than 1,200 men and women of all backgrounds and ages. In the midst of her research she came across the following passage from a speech by Theodore Roosevelt, which the former US president delivered in the spring of 1910 in Paris, about a year after leaving office. Roosevelt's speech, alternately titled "Citizenship in a Republic" or "The Man in the Arena," describes people who have the courage to show up for challenges:

"It is not the critic who counts; not the man who points out how the strong man stumbles, or where the doer of deeds could have done them better. The credit belongs to the man who is actually in the arena, whose face is marred by dust and sweat and blood; who strives valiantly; who errs, who comes short again and again, because there is no effort without error and shortcoming, but who does actually strive to do the deeds; who knows great enthusiasms, the great devotions; who spends himself in a worthy cause; who at the best knows in the end the triumph of high achievement, and who at the worst, if he fails, at least fails while daring greatly . . ."

– Theodore Roosevelt

In *Daring Greatly*, Brown links Roosevelt's idea to the premise that people must embrace their vulnerability in order to live in a way that allows them to feel worthy, connected, and authentic. She subscribes to the idea that life is not about winning or losing, but about having the courage to enter the arena and engage with life.

1

SCARCITY: LOOKING INSIDE OUR CULTURE OF "NEVER ENOUGH"

Overview

In the first chapter of *Daring Greatly*, Brené Brown shares her perception that many people today are struggling with the belief that they are not good enough to be worthy of love and connection. In fact, she says, this collective belief is so strong that it is actually reshaping our culture. The shame created by feelings of unworthiness is giving rise to anger, disconnection, blame, and dangerous forms of comparison, conditions that create a culture of *scarcity*.

According to Brown, people's belief that they are not enough, and do not have enough, spills over into their workplaces, affects their social lives, and causes distress within their families. The way to counteract this condition, she says, is to cultivate *Wholeheartedness*. Brown defines this quality as willingness to be vulnerable and to feel a sense of self-worth in the face of uncertainty and risk.

Chapter Summary

Brené Brown notes that people today seem more self-centered than they did in previous generations. She observes that much of this apparent self-centeredness is blamed on social media sites like Facebook, where people share mundane details of their lives, believing that the information will be interesting to everyone. This may look like an epidemic of narcissism, but Brown posits that what's really going on is a culture-wide experience of the *shame-based fear of being ordinary*. She believes that people don't feel special enough to be noticed, and they don't feel worthy enough to belong or be loved. When people adopt seemingly narcissistic behaviors, it is not because they have a giant ego or lack sensitivity, but because they want to meet societal expectations, protect themselves, and avoid looking vulnerable. Diagnosing apparently self-centered behavior as narcissism only perpetuates the problem by stigmatizing a large segment of the population while doing nothing to address the root problem. Instead, Brown says, this kind of behavior should be seen through a more human lens, the *lens of vulnerability*.

According to Brown, one of the most powerful struggles in contemporary United States culture is the struggle with feelings of scarcity. Brown says that these feelings stem in part from recent traumatic experiences, including the 9/11 attacks, the wars in Iraq and Afghanistan, the Great Recession, and increases in random violence. These traumas have led to reactions of anger and fear, and accompanying perceptions of scarcity. People imagine that life would be more fulfilling if only they could be better and have more. This manifests in the desire to be thinner, smarter, richer, or kinder, among other attributes. People judge their "ordinary" lives as inadequate because of unrealistic, self-damaging comparisons with the lives of others—the wealthy, the famous, or even just the neighbors.

Brown divides people's struggle with scarcity into three components: shame, comparison, and disengagement. She believes that shame has permeated daily life, revealing itself in behaviors like lashing out at others or hiding to avoid connection. When people compare themselves to others on the basis of standards that are impossible to meet, they sacrifice their creativity. People try to protect themselves by disengaging from life and refusing to be vulnerable.

Brené Brown writes that the opposite of living in scarcity is living with the idea of "enough"—what she calls living in Wholeheartedness. When people face uncertainty and discomfort with courage, allowing themselves to be vulnerable and willing to fail, they are able to maintain a strong sense of personal worthiness. A Wholehearted life has to be lived day by day, Brown says, because people receive so many messages of scarcity. Those messages can be challenged, but first it is necessary to address a number of myths concerning vulnerability—the topic of *Daring Greatly*'s second chapter.

Chapter 1: Key Points

- In the past decade, members of US culture have suffered through a number of traumas—terrorist attacks, wars, natural disasters, random violence—and these have resulted in an epidemic of post-traumatic stress, which manifests as a sense of *scarcity*.

- Scarcity is driven by shame and fear; people feel that they aren't good enough and don't have enough. This notion is reinforced by people's tendency to compare their lives to a fictional ideal in which other people know more, have more, and live better.

- To counteract scarcity, it is necessary to practice living in a state of *Wholeheartedness*, which requires the courage to be vulnerable, and even to fail, but still feel worthy of love and connection.

2

DEBUNKING THE VULNERABILITY MYTHS

Overview

According to Brené Brown, there are four pervasive myths about vulnerability: that vulnerability is weakness, that people can choose not to be vulnerable, that vulnerability means revealing everything to everybody, and that it is possible for someone to go it alone. This chapter puts those notions to rest.

Chapter Summary

Myth #1: Vulnerability Is Weakness

According to Brown, many people see vulnerability simply as weakness. It is not uncommon for vulnerable people to be held in contempt for being too emotional, and meanwhile the courage behind their vulnerability remains unseen or ignored. But vulnerability and feeling are inseparable, Brown says, and to deny one is to deny the other. The willingness to acknowledge and act on painful, uncomfortable, or frightening feelings is an act of bravery. Vulnerability is not just associated with negative emotions; it is also where love, empathy, creativity, and courage can be found. Brown notes that the path to Wholeheartedness requires learning to engage with all of these feelings—and throughout that process, weakness is nowhere to be found.

Myth #2: "I Don't Do Vulnerability"

Being vulnerable means experiencing uncertainty, taking risks, and being emotionally exposed. As such, Brown says, many people try to avoid vulnerability so they can remain in the apparent safety and predictability of their personal comfort zones. However, the act of living involves various degrees of emotional exposure, whether one chooses it or not. Denial of this reality results in unhealthy responses to risk and uncertainty, including fear, anger, judgment, and efforts to exert control, impose perfection, or manufacture certainty. Brown believes that it is damaging to put on a suit of armor in an effort to protect what ultimately cannot be protected. If people are open and vulnerable in uncomfortable situations instead, they will be more likely to find their way to engagement and connection.

Myth #3: Vulnerability Is Letting It All Hang Out

Brown writes that practicing vulnerability does not mean revealing everything publicly or sharing intimate details with strangers. In fact, Brown describes this type of behavior as the opposite of vulnerability. Instead, true vulnerability occurs when people share personal feelings and experiences with a trusted listener, someone with whom a solid relationship exists. This kind of relationship is built carefully over time through small but significant moments of connection that establish trust. The possibility of betrayal and abandonment is always present, Brown notes, but revealing vulnerability to a trusted person is more likely to strengthen the existing bond.

Myth #4: We Can Go It Alone

The concept of a lone individual struggling unaided through the landscape of life may be attractive, but it is unrealistic. Brown believes going it alone is not possible for someone who seeks to live Wholeheartedly. People need support, encouragement, and counsel when they take risks. They also need the courage to be vulnerable enough to ask for help.

Chapter 2: Key Points

- Vulnerability is not a sign of weakness. It takes strength and courage to be open to feelings that are painful and difficult to navigate.

- It is understandable that some people try to eliminate risk, uncertainty, and exposure by limiting vulnerability, but these elements of life cannot be avoided.

- Vulnerability does not mean sharing intimate details with strangers. That is just a way to avoid real vulnerability, which takes place between people who have established trust and boundaries.

- The solitary figure going it alone is a romantic notion. A vulnerable life is lived with others' support, to be vulnerable, and even to fail, but still feel worthy of love and connection.

3

UNDERSTANDING AND COMBATING SHAME

Overview

Brené Brown defines shame as the fear of being disconnected from everyone else, and of being pushed away and isolated. It is a painful emotion that awakens the primitive "lizard brain" fight-or-flight response. To overcome the effects of shame, Brown recommends techniques for *shame resilience*—four "moves," or elements, of what she calls "Gremlin Ninja Warrior training." Brown says that shame creates the silence that shuts down vulnerability, but breaking that silence can bring vulnerability back.

Chapter Summary

According to Brené Brown, shame is the fear that a particular action or failure will cause one to be disconnected from everyone else. She notes that almost everyone in every culture feels shame, most frequently with regard to body image, money, parenthood, family, health, addiction, sex, aging, religion, trauma, and being labeled. Shame is a common human emotion, Brown says, because humans are hardwired to need connection. She describes the fear of losing that connection as literally painful, often to the same degree as serious physical pain.

Brown sees shame as one of the most effective blocks to creativity, innovation, feedback, and connection. Shame encourages silence, smallness, and disconnection, she says. It prevents people from taking risks as it shrinks and eliminates self-worth.

Brown notes that shame is usually learned in childhood, when parents and teachers with good intentions voice the criticisms that will play themselves out again and again when children become adults. Brown has a name for these internalized critical voices: *gremlins*. The gremlins, she says, are continually at work to undermine self-confidence, feelings of worthiness, and the capacity for vulnerability.

Because shame thrives in darkness and silence, Brown says, one powerful way to undermine it and fight the gremlins is to bring it into the light and talk about it. She believes that shame tends to vanish once it has been exposed. Unfortunately, though, most people are terrified to talk about shame, and that reluctance gives it even more power.

According to Brown, before feelings of shame can be talked about, the word "shame" has to be properly distinguished from some other terms that are commonly confused with it. For instance, the words "guilt" and "shame" are often considered interchangeable, but guilt is specific to a particular action, not to a way of being. The difference between guilt and shame, Brown says, is the difference between telling a misbehaving child "Your behavior is bad" and telling the child "You are bad." Brown sees guilt as a helpful tool for pointing out when actions are not aligned with values. Guilt has a positive influence, she says, whereas shame has the opposite effect: it corrodes feelings of self-worth and connection, leading to outcomes like depression, addiction, and aggression. "Humiliation" is another word often interchanged with the word "shame." Brown notes that the difference is that people don't believe they deserve to be humiliated, but when people feel shame, they believe they deserve to feel that way.

Brown says that shame causes real pain, which triggers people's fight-or-flight response. When people lack the cognitive tools for recognizing and counteracting the effects of shame, they employ various strategies to stop the pain. These strategies include withdrawal, appeasement, and aggression, Brown says, but they work mostly at the expense of connection. Brown believes that there's a better way to counteract the often devastating effects of shame, and she suggests learning the four techniques of *shame resilience*:

1. Identify feelings and triggers of shame.
2. Determine whether others' expectations and values are causing shame.
3. Seek an empathetic ear.
4. Talk about feelings of shame.

When it comes to shame, men and women have different experiences, Brown says. Women tend to feel shame with regard to body image and personal appearance, motherhood, and the pressure to effortlessly "have it all." Women are subject to the cultural expectation that they should focus on their appearance and put others' happiness before their own. Men, however, experience shame with regard to perceived weakness, which is often tied to their ability to be vulnerable. This situation is made more confusing by the fact that women often ask men to be vulnerable, but recoil if men comply. According to Brown, women who feel shame often respond with provocation and criticism, while men tend to respond with anger or silence. But the way out of the shame conundrum for everyone is to practice vulnerability—to cultivate intimacy and connection.

Chapter 3: Key Points

- Shame is the fear of losing connection with people—
  of being left alone and isolated. It is as painful as any
  physical injury, and it is a universal human emotion.

- Women feel shame primarily around the issues of
  appearance and parenting, and they tend to respond with
  criticism. Men feel shame primarily around their perceived
  weakness, and they react with either anger or silence.

- Shame operates in darkness, and it thrives on silence. To
  counteract its toxic effects, it is important to recognize its
  triggers and to talk about it with trusted, empathetic people.

THE VULNERABILITY ARMORY

Overview

Brené Brown sees adolescence as the time in life when people begin to develop a variety of masks to cover up their vulnerability, which can suddenly seem frightening. By the time adulthood arrives, Brown says, the average person has collected a virtual arsenal of individually tailored shields and weapons to protect against the perceived dangers of vulnerability. Brown's research shows that several types of shields are common to almost everyone. She calls these shields *common vulnerability armor*.

Chapter Summary

From the time of adolescence, according to Brené Brown, people develop personality masks and shields to protect themselves from vulnerability. Many of these are unique to an individual's own suffering, but some forms of armor are universal, she says. Brown discusses eight kinds of shields in this chapter. Here are the three most common types:

1. *Foreboding joy* is an experience in which something extremely positive—for example, the birth of a child, the start of a romantic relationship, or appreciation of a great job or a loving spouse—is accompanied by an image of impending

doom or disaster. Joy can be a doorway to vulnerability, Brown says, so people imagine disaster as a way to shield themselves from feeling vulnerable. For Brown, whether foreboding appears in the form of *rehearsing tragedy* (playing out disastrous scenarios in the mind) or *feeling perpetual disappointment* (not allowing joy), it is always born from the feeling of scarcity. The sense of not having enough joy will lead to painful disappointment, she says, and so foreboding keeps prospective pain at bay. To overcome foreboding, Brown recommends practicing gratitude for joyous moments, for ordinary moments that include family members and friends, and for other sources of joy.

2. Brown sees *perfectionism* as a way to shield vulnerability by seeking approval (through fear of criticism) and avoiding shame (through fear of failure). But perfectionism, Brown says, creates feelings of inadequacy and scarcity: since perfection can never be achieved, the search for it becomes self-destructive and addictive. As a way out of perfectionism, Brown advises learning to identify and appreciate personal imperfections and practicing self-kindness. Suffering is universal, Brown says, and so it's important for people to "live inside" their personal stories and to own the incidents, positive and negative, of their lives.

3. Brown sees the shield of *numbing* at work in our culture's record-high rates of obesity, drug use, debt, and addiction. She believes that these outcomes are due to so many people's attempts to shield their vulnerability with behavior whose ultimate purpose is to deaden feelings. But Brown also points out that there are people who have developed strong boundaries and learned to act only in ways that are aligned

with their values, saying no to everything else. To determine whether a particular type of behavior is actually intended to numb feelings, Brown advises being mindful of the intention behind eating, drinking, taking prescription or recreational drugs, or taking on too much work.

In addition to the common vulnerability armor of foreboding joy, perfectionism, and numbing, Brown describes five less common types of shields:

1. The *Viking-or-victim worldview,* a shield recognizable by a person's belief that all people can be divided into two mutually exclusive groups: those who are constantly being taken advantage of, and those who are always in control and must win at all costs. As a way out of this mindset, Brown advises nurturing trust and connection.

2. *Floodlighting* is what Brown calls one form of oversharing—in this case, confiding intimate details to people who are not trusted friends, in the hope of creating a connection without first cultivating a relationship. Brown sees floodlighting as in instance of misusing vulnerability. She recommends not sharing intimate or painful stories with anyone but trusted friends or family members. Otherwise, she says, the story is liable to repulse the listener and create even more disconnection.

3. For Brown, another form of oversharing is the *smash-and-grab job,* which Brown compares to a burglar's smashing in a door or a window and grabbing whatever is at hand. She calls this move "sloppy, unplanned, and desperate," not unlike the actions of a clumsy invader. Floodlighting

misuses vulnerability for the sake of connection; by contrast, the smash-and-grab maneuver uses vulnerability as a tool of manipulation, smashing through conventional social boundaries for the purpose of stealing other people's attention and energy. Again, Brown says, to overcome this kind of behavior, a helpful first step is to discern the real intention behind it.

4. Brown describes *serpentining* as emotionally running in a zigzag pattern away from a vulnerable situation—bouncing from distraction to distraction as a way to seek avoidance. To remove this shield, Brown recommends being present, recognizing the behavior, trying not to take it too seriously, and simply moving forward.

5. Brown lists *cynicism, criticism, cool,* and *cruelty* not only as shields against vulnerability but also as weapons used against those who display vulnerability. People who wield these weapons are threatened and shamed by their own inability to display vulnerability. Nevertheless, Brown says, it is important to stay open to useful criticism and feedback while also finding ways not to be crushed by people whose fear and shame prompt them to use criticism as a weapon.

Chapter 4: Key Points

- People begin developing emotional shields at an early age to protect themselves from the fear and uncertainty of vulnerability. By the time people become adults, it is often difficult for them to know who they really are beneath their *common vulnerability armor.*

- The use of three types of emotional shields—*foreboding joy, perfectionism,* and *numbing*—is nearly universal. Other shields include adopting the *Viking-or-victim worldview,* oversharing in the form of *floodlighting* or the *smash-and-grab job, serpentining* to escape a vulnerable situation, and defensive uses of *cynicism, criticism, cool,* and *cruelty.*

- The techniques of Wholeheartedness, which include nurturing self-kindness, mindfulness, and paying attention, can be used to pry these shields away and release the genuine, vulnerable self.

5

MIND THE GAP: CULTIVATING CHANGE AND CLOSING THE DISENGAGEMENT DIVIDE

Overview

The value gap, as Brené Brown defines it in this chapter, is the distance between the values to which people aspire and the values that people actually put into practice. The existence of this gap leads to disengagement, which Brown describes as a shield against vulnerability and shame. For Brown, paying attention to the value gap, and closing it by making a conscious effort to practice *aspirational values*, both lowers the shield of disengagement and nurtures vulnerability.

Chapter Summary

In this chapter, Brené Brown refers to the "Mind the Gap" sign used in the London subway system to warn riders about not falling into the space between the platform and the train. Brown calls attention to another kind of gap, the value gap, which looms between aspirational values (representing what people want to do and who people want to be) and actual values (representing what is actually done and who people actually are). The pain and the shame of the value gap can lead to disengagement, a vulnerability shield that Brown holds responsible for most of the problems now facing businesses, families, and communities.

Brown sees disengagement as the culprit when people in leadership positions (such as politicians, clergy, and even parents) fail to live up to the expectations of those who look to them for guidance. To take one of the examples that Brown offers, politicians make laws that they themselves often break with impunity while pointing the finger at each other. As another example, Brown notes that many religions use a "compliance and consequences" model, taking advantage of followers' fear and uncertainty instead of modeling a more loving and accepting approach to spirituality. She also lists examples of disconnections between parental values and practices:

- A mother expects her children to be honest, but she fails to notify a store when she is inadvertently not charged for soda.
- A father insists on respect and accountability from his sons, but he is too busy to talk with them when they argue about a broken toy.
- Parents demand gratitude and respect from their children, but they model ungrateful and disrespectful behavior not just toward their children but also toward each other.
- Parents preach about the importance of limits, but they regale their teenager with tales of their own substance abuse and wild behavior in their teenage years.

But Brown also includes the example of parents who not only preach but also practice the values of emotional connection and honored feelings. When these parents' teenage boy comes home from school and is obviously upset, they drop what they're doing, sit down, and share with him their own emotional struggles that they remember from their school years.

To begin closing the value gap, and to rediscover the vulnerability that Brené Brown sees as essential to Wholeheartedness, Brown says it is important to pay close attention to how well aspirations are aligned with daily practice. Perfection is not the goal, she says; instead, the goal is to be willing to show up every day and make an effort. Brown offers a timely reminder here: the "gremlins" mentioned in chapter 3 are more than likely to make an appearance when the work of rediscovering vulnerability is under way. Again, Brown says, paying attention is the key to success.

Chapter 5: Key Points

- Disengagement occurs when there is a gap between the values that an individual, an organization, and/or a community aspires to practice and the values that the individual, organization, and/or community actually does practice.

- This disengagement creates shame, pain, and uncertainty— feelings that cause people to hide their vulnerability behind a shield of even more disengagement.

- People can restore vulnerability by paying close daily attention to the difference between the values they espouse and those they actually practice.

6

DISRUPTIVE ENGAGEMENT: DARING TO REHUMANIZE EDUCATION AND WORK

Overview

Brené Brown writes that it is risky to introduce innovations or creative ideas, because doing so opens up the very real possibility of ridicule and failure. Yet creativity and innovation are needed today more than ever, she says, and they must be encouraged and nourished in organizations, schools, religious institutions, and families. According to Brown, in order for creativity and innovation to be reinvigorated in a culture, it is necessary to recognize and address the way shame manifests in that culture. Innovation and creativity prosper in cultures where blame and finger-pointing are discouraged and people are encouraged to give and receive feedback, even when it is uncomfortable.

Chapter Summary

Brené Brown observes that people who dare to be innovative and creative are also willing to risk derision and failure. Most people keep to themselves, though, since they're too fearful of shame and uncertainty to make themselves vulnerable. To counteract this tendency at work, Brown suggests *rehumanizing* the dehumanized workplace by recognizing and naming notions of scarcity, nurturing vulnerability, and overturning shame.

Because shame in the workplace leads to fear, Brown writes, it can subvert and sabotage not only creativity and innovation but also productivity. She reiterates that shame works in the shadows, which is why it is not always easy to recognize when shame has begun to permeate an organization. Brown says that a sure sign that shame has become embedded in a culture is when shame is used as a method of control, punishment, or manipulation. This often happens at work because so many people have been shamed by their families from a young age; as a result, they see shame as an effective management technique, and they carry it into the workplace. Brown warns that once shame-based management reaches a certain saturation point, people begin to disengage as a method of self-protection. This kind of disengagement is directly implicated in producing employees who lie, cheat, steal, or desperately seek new employment.

"If blame is driving," Brown says, "shame is riding shotgun." According to Brown, when blame has become a cultural pattern, shame has to be sought out and uprooted. For example, if protecting an organization's reputation has become more important than respecting the basic human dignity of its employees, then shame is driving the organization's agenda.

Brown believes it is more important than ever to develop creativity, innovation, and problem solving in every corner of society, which can be done only by encouraging engagement. Brown recommends four strategies for stimulating engagement and overturning a culture of shame:

1. Support leaders who are honest and who are willing to stop shaming in the workplace.
2. Take a close, hard look at where shame may be operating in organizations.
3. Ask people to share their experiences of struggle.
4. Teach people about the difference between guilt and shame.

Another way to address and mitigate shame, Brown says, is to encourage the kind of feedback that promotes transformation and change. Giving and receiving feedback can be a difficult experience, and so it's not always easy to promote clear, honest feedback within a culture. But, Brown says, the goal in initiating a feedback program should not be to eliminate but to *normalize* discomfort, since real growth and change are almost always uncomfortable. Thus, she says, one way to take anxiety, fear, and shame out of giving and receiving feedback is to let people know that discomfort is a normal part of the process.

In creating a culture of feedback, it can be helpful to assess people's difficulties from the perspective of their strengths, Brown says. She sees this approach as a way to reveal what is possible for people in terms of their particular talents and abilities. When people's strengths and limitations are examined at the same time, their strengths can be used to address their limitations.

For Brown, a culture that employs feedback in this way is a culture that nurtures vulnerability for both the person who receives the feedback and the person who provides it. This kind of engaged feedback process promotes a positive situation Brown calls "sitting on the same side of the table."

Chapter 6: Key Points

- At every level of society, innovation and creativity are more important than ever. However, most people play it safe and keep quiet, since they're so afraid of risking the ridicule and failure that sharing new and creative ideas may invite.

- In any culture—a company's, a school's, or a family's—the use of blame to manipulate and control people is a sign that shame is in charge.

- Clear, honest feedback can be uncomfortable—*and it should be uncomfortable*, since real growth and change will always involve at least some discomfort. But even if feedback is an occasion for discomfort, it never has to be an occasion for shame.

7

WHOLEHEARTED PARENTING: DARING TO BE THE ADULTS WE WANT OUR CHILDREN TO BE

Overview

Being a parent is one of the most challenging and difficult things to do, Brené Brown says, largely because it presents so many opportunities for shame, blame, and failure. She believes that although parents are always trying to find the best techniques for bringing up their children, what matters most in the end is who the parent is and how the parent behaves. Therefore, it is important for parents to practice vulnerability, openness, compassion, and empathy, not only toward their children but also toward themselves. There is no such thing as the perfect parent, Brown writes, but when parents model Wholehearted behavior, they can teach their children to be Wholehearted themselves.

Chapter Summary

Brené Brown sees most parents as having the same goal: bringing their children up to be Wholehearted people. Getting to that goal can be a frightening journey, since the uncertainty involved in parenting creates vast potential for shame and judgment.

Brown believes that parenting techniques have much less bearing on how children turn out than parents' identity and demonstrated behavior. For this reason, difficult though it is, parents have to stay vulnerable. Parenting should be about loving and accepting, not about knowing and proving.

Parents can't give their children what they themselves don't have, Brown writes, so parents have to learn to love and accept themselves before they can teach their children to do the same. Children learn what they experience, she says.

Many people believe that they will not be worthy until they have fulfilled certain requirements—losing weight, getting a promotion, buying a house, and so on—and Brown notes that parents are no exception to this common pattern. But this thinking pattern encourages shame, which tends to get handed down from parents to their children. This is particularly true when it comes to gender-specific messages; for example, girls get the message that they should be thin, nice, and quiet, and boys get the message that they should be strong, aggressive, and high-earners.

Another common hand-me-down from parents to children is perfectionism, according to Brown. From the practice of perfectionism, children learn to place more importance on what other people think than on their own thoughts and feelings. Brown offers the example of a little girl walking into a room where her parents are sitting. Do her parents let their faces show love and acceptance, or do their faces betray judgment of the child's appearance? A parent's expression is a subtle but important signal to a child, Brown says. Is it necessary for the child to look right before her parents will be loving and accepting, or does the child feel cherished just by walking into the room?

Brown stresses the importance of paying attention to what children are told about *themselves*, as opposed to what they are told about their *behavior.* For example, if a child is told that he *did something* bad, that message creates guilt, and guilt can help him change his behavior; but if he's told that *he is* bad, that message creates shame, and shame can lead to outcomes like depression, addiction, and violence.

According to Brown, when parents teach their children the difference between shame and guilt, they can help their children recognize shame when they encounter it in the world outside the home. In other words, teaching children the difference between shame and guilt aids in instilling and strengthening shame resilience in children. It is also important, Brown notes, to tell children that they are not alone in their struggles with shame, and that everyone experiences such struggles.

Brown emphasizes the importance of knowing the difference between fitting in and belonging. Fitting in, she writes, means figuring out who to be in order to be accepted, while belonging means not having to be someone else in order to be accepted. Children need to know that they belong in their family no matter who they are or what they do. In order to instill this knowledge in their children, parents, too, need to know that they belong in their family no matter who they are or what they do.

Another important parental skill, Brown says, is letting go and allowing children to experience situations independently. If children are to develop a strong sense of hope, they must be allowed to confront difficult issues, as appropriate, without parental intervention. Parents need to know when to let go and let their children experience disappointment, conflict, and failure on their own.

Brown believes that being a parent is one of the most challenging, uncertain things anyone can do. However, if parents pay attention to values, do their best to remain vulnerable and present, and model Wholehearted behavior, they can be Wholehearted themselves while also showing their children how to live in a Wholehearted way.

Chapter 7: Key Points

- There is no such thing as the perfect parent, and no one particular technique of parenting is likely to produce children who grow up to be happy, secure, self-assured individuals.

- Although it is crucial for parents to support their children, it is equally important for parents to know when offering support crosses the line into being overprotective. Children who are never free of parental intervention are not free to engage in appropriate struggles with their own disappointments, conflicts, and failures, and they're also not free to develop their own strengths and sense of hope.

- When parents model Wholehearted behavior— vulnerability, compassion, empathy, and acceptance— children can learn how to practice Wholeheartedness in their own lives.

CONCLUSION

Brené Brown, a researcher in the areas of shame and vulnerability, believes that US culture has become a culture of scarcity, one in which people feel that nothing they have and nothing they do will ever be enough. Brown sees this feeling of scarcity as having led to a current epidemic of shame, fear, and disconnection in all sectors of society. As a result, she says, many people have lost all motivation even to show up, much less "dare greatly," in what Theodore Roosevelt called "the arena." They no longer feel willing or able to face the challenges, great and small, of participating fully in life.

But Brown also believes that people can find their way out of scarcity and shame, and back into a state of Wholeheartedness, by returning to the practice of vulnerability. Since vulnerability opens people to fear and uncertainty, it is often mistaken for weakness. Brown upends common myths about vulnerability and reveals that it is actually a measure of strength.

Throughout the book, Brown emphasizes the importance of recognizing how people arm themselves against vulnerability, how they create gaps between their ideal values and the values they actually practice, and how that kind of behavior tends to dehumanize both the individual and the larger culture. When people allow themselves to be vulnerable and live Wholeheartedly, Brown says, they can also model Wholeheartedness for others and help to create a healthier and more accepting culture.

APPENDIX

A Note on the Author's Research Process

Brené Brown reports that she initially intended to find empirical evidence of what she already knew to be true about vulnerability. She soon discovered that in order to address what really mattered to her research participants, she would need to conduct *grounded theory research*, an approach in which new theory is developed on the basis of actual experience rather than on the basis of existing theory. In other words, Brown had to let her research participants define the research problems, then relinquish her own ideas and trust that what emerged would be correct. She found herself employing techniques in her research that are also used to achieve Wholeheartedness—openness, acceptance, and engagement.

Brown set out at first to study connection, but she discovered that the participants were very afraid of *dis*connection. They feared that they were somehow unworthy of connection. She discovered that such fears may be resolved through the practices of vulnerability, compassion, and empathy. She encountered participants who were managing to remain vulnerable and live Wholeheartedly, despite fear and uncertainty.

For her research, Brown interviewed 750 women between the ages of eighteen and eighty-eight, with an average age of forty-one. Of this group, 43 percent were Caucasian, 30 percent were African American, 18 percent were Latina, and 8 percent were Asian. Brown also interviewed 530 men whose average age was forty-eight. Of the male participants, 40 percent were Caucasian, 25 percent were African American, 20 percent were Latino, and 15 percent were Asian.